CW00457090

# IN THE VILLAGE THAT IS NOT BURNING DOWN

# IN THE VILLAGE THAT IS NOT BURNING DOWN

*poems*

## TRAVIS NATHAN BROWN

*atmosphere press*

© 2021 Travis Nathan Brown

Published by Atmosphere Press

Cover design by Senhor Tocas

No part of this book may be reproduced without permission from the author except in brief quotations and in reviews.

atmospherepress.com

# Contents

## HENCE

It [the town] has never had any sizable factories.

—WILLIAM MAXWELL

Of the family
By the family
For the family

—ABE LINCOLN

# WHENCE

# THE ROPE ADVANCES

Attention winches, capstans,
all you nubile come-a-longs,

the mechanical advantages entreat you.

In tugs, in cinches, come
late hangers-on, hang on,

pull this, my pull-strength,
test my sisal, noose my jute.

Call up the dealer of pulley-wheels

and wind me, my tensile tree,
my cordage coiled, kinked,

your levers entwined in my length.

# SONG FOR A PLUMMETING YOUNG MACHINE

Out of the mother
stoked with coal.
Out of the shake,

rattle and roll.
Out of traction,
and into the train

off the track
and on its back.

And into the ravine,
into the deep, making
quick and telltale squeaks,

into the gorge
the cargo goes—

green eggs and grenadine,
the haberdashery,
its fancy handkerchiefs,

the roasted beets,
napkins and knives,
and finally, the tired
diapers, the swine,

and the merlot.

Out of the forgettable,
and into the shit-faced future,
into its ever-erupting parade,

and into this undone
day that won't shut up.

Into the ramparts, over and over,
and into this orange applause,

this ovation of diesel, its fire,
the sound of one hand clapping.

Out of the father,
out of the steam,
out of the river wide.

Out of him,
this and that
scribbled sky.

And into this
high-up thing,
where a god
might hang,

flexing his beefcakes,
and polishing his
bishop's bouffant.

Out of all that,
and into this
falling caboose,

into its wrenching
music, into
its pollutant,

into this plummeting
song, and into its
blooming bruises.

While the dust dances around.
While the treetops twist all willy-nilly.
While the river jives idly by.

And deeper still,
into the rest of this
mess, landing then, on

and into its feet,
into the whole lot, into
its hot, and into its juice.

Onward and further and tally-ho,
into this kind of unnecessary delicacy,
into its home you go.

# A ROMANTIC IN A LOOSE LAND

Let's touch
our playthings &
hurry away the incurable

the past like
an infection
it goes on discharging that

loose clap
in the round
the rabble roused almost sung

the chorus too
beautiful
how the mouth moves across

the flesh
of a word
pushing forward so it falls from

the roof
to the floor
what we hear it aspirates like

an aerosol
what we say
what we think that is memory

that's not
science science
is a motion a mother closing

the curtains
in the big world
a mother drawing the night

      into her thick
arms again
   we never touch that empty

      cradle that
deep rocking
   like an aquifer under an ill

      plowed Midwest
that big shot
   of water from who knows

      to what is
mud & stone
   dim's dark nameable same as

      any cloud
blowing any
   wet's rain ends well is well

      a slippery place

# HALF-PAST POLECAT HILL

what is home: sky & wood a pile of yellow flicker the
figure inside: a piano: carved out or cored through: the
apple: no Adam no how: it nettles: I do recall whatever
dancing is: is what the dancer does: legs & poses
junction &: flow: that discontinuous signature: if not
now: then: when it roils: sung in streaks of plumage: in
the baying of a dog up is: whatever rose: whatever saw:

## HENRI LAMOTHE DIVES OFF THE FLATIRON
## BUILDING INTO TWELVE INCHES OF WATER

*(heft & heave)*

On holidays
in the early '60s
Henri would give rides
on his big belly, pushing
the guts, practicing the flop:
his chest half-emptied,
dreaming the high dive,
the shallow pool,
the giving body.

★

*(belt of wine)*

A punishment
unto water,
he never failed
to hit it hard,

opening once
for Evel Knievel
at the Wembley
Circus, living

by the arch
of his back,
by his belly,
that bulge

like karate,
chopping
twelve & one
quarter inches

of sweetness,
that stiff
water, a belt
of wine.

★

*(etymology)*

someone
who lived
in a fortified
stronghold of
Old French
*motte*

of Gaulish
origin
a hillock
or mound see
also
*moat*

the definite
article *la*
surname
habitational
a name from
the several

places named
with this
feminine
word lump
a clod of earth
or a block
of butter

★

*(mark & miss)*

Henri was
the hurt
in the water

refusing
just once
to hit it

too much
wind in Kansas
the time

he dropped that
sack of charcoal
like a myth

it couldn't deal
with the
concrete

★

*(tunnel of air)*

After shows
children ask if
it hurts him
& Henri asks them

*Why do you care if it hurts?*

A dream
is a dive
from the Eiffel
Tower that
tunnel of air

# POEM IN WHICH A MAN TAKES A BATH

Look—
I unhinge
a blue

sloop
flapping
like a saxophone

I toot
to the beyond
to the embarcadero

ahoy!
my green sails
bibbidi-boppidi-boo

this skiff's
a rowing
to the mouth of

the undertow
that suck
of want to

I go
to dishwater
to sink

scum
like poison
old friend

I float in this
big tub
but I feel

too heavy
like a total
nobody

# THIRD-DEGREE LITANY

*for Oren Dietrich Brown*

When his best guesses are vice grips and wrenches and fly
strips and his clothes are and his heart must have and the
sink is and the swirling eye of blood is a sea he walks on
when the garage door is a brick and it is dropping in his
pocket a man in the river and whenever he grips the
steering wheel's hide it sings *flesh of the body* and the flood
comes across the dash and like a new tooth the ivory
Chrysler shines and not a blade of grass is standing out of
place but there will be and the next and there is and if it's
close enough the shoe still fits though it doesn't when his
son comes walking over the plank and all anyone can say is
so long sitting in a chair and torn from the wall the
telephone is the face of a father and it is saying       *hello*

## SOME BIRDS WON'T FLY

He said I was faster than
the heat deep in the hardest
dark cranny of grassland.

Hell, I believed the dead
danced in the weed tree
windbreaks. He showed me

the tight kites of organdy
and I tangled there. I guess
it was a breeze that carried

me after him. I clutched up
the motherless chicks and hid
my loot low in the bramble.

Sugar, I coughed, and every
sweet need knuckled me,
it cracked my panting animal

like an egg on the stovetop.
I could not forget his ghost
in the bold-cold henhouses,

the ten-acre field of ragweed
the boys burned on purpose.
Not long after the concrete

men smoothed into a gray lake its
foundation, the house sunk in,
and the heavy bird nested there.

# THE LOVE MANUFACTURING COMPANY

agriculture
is to

machinery

as
lumber is

to coal

harvester
is to slaughter

as slaughter is

to house
house is to

manufacture

as a hand
is to facture

facture is

to make
as make is

to love

## A ROOM IN THE ELEPHANT

My big brother—you know I love him—his wife died horribly, & now he is planting peanuts in the bedroom closet. The soil is deep & sandy there, & that's good for the peanuts. If you look hard enough, you'll find everything you ever wanted in a word. Like how *peanut* means *under earth*.

# A HUNDRED THOUSAND HOLLOW LEGS

After the first leg filled with melted snow, we sat around nearly broken over it, watching the paint peel, the wallpaper slumping to the floor. In one leg lay our mother, in another, our papa, that son of a tall drink of water. We were all set on a course stricken with curses— even the preachers suffered spells. During the nine-year hiccup, the town filled four or five hundred more, crowded them with remedies, the useless, spooky ones. Later there was a leg that clattered with flatware. Another bulged with the feast of fat kings. One leg had no secrets at all. It was the worst. When the goddamn phone rang, it was the middle of the night, and the ringing filled up another one. At one point, everyone was shouting, shaking the green trees or beating the black sheets, and it was only morning. We looked up to the mountain, but the mountain was the sky. Our judgment was terrible, our disappointment just right. We made sure there was never any pleasing us. The next leg we sowed with its own weakening, its red meat soon riddled, twisted and turned into lemons. We packed another with grand occasions, big scissors, the mayor and the ribbon. One leg held a bulldozer; another held the black earth, the kinky worms, their pink magic. We couldn't help them. In one leg, there was a shallow grave. It held many small swans and the slender neck of our dead daughter. In another, we laid her sweet teeth on top of some candy apples. Only one leg brimmed with our sighing, the good and the bad. Inside one, a Ferris wheel spun, and a little happiness twirled there, its dizziness tickled the air, and so the passengers went, their legs dangling, some of them crammed with baby hair, some with bits of poorly thought-out heartache, others loaded with lost battles, failing factories, or shrinking towns. If one throbbed with snakes, another held their missing legs, and the big wheel, it kept on turning.

# THE KICKAPOO CHINA COMPANY

fire

destroyed
everything

except
for the kilns

they withstood it
pointing at

the obvious sky
much like

fire

## MONOLOGUE AFTER A MOSTLY
## UNAPPARENT KINGDOM COME

Maybe it just
glided by I guess
nothing sticks to
a green glass city
we didn't think
it would our plan
was a dark hat no
sleep two bats so
it must have been
hers mine got sick
of bright lights big
deal put a hard one
under those great
glad moustaches
the heart is just
an apple and I'm
not a touched on
jerk up a tender
tree but a bird you
see we did break
in it was just us
me and her both
cut him like that
and now we worry
each day first thing
it's like a knife
you can stick it
into anything

# WRITING LARRY LINGO:
# À LA TEENAGE THEATER

I wrote:    how language spilled into us: or: over you:
            alphabetical scum: dirt: baggage-sick: sick
            of spelling: x & y: the love lots: of words:
            I couldn't even think: of sputum of youth
            of ganged brothers: if cut up: in half: what
            boiled in me: what in each was inside me:
            what was: yolky: a smear: maybe hope was:
            wicked: scrambling: what was: say it: the
            past: by a nose: a whiff: of getting hit: in a
            car: by red boxing: a glove: that old
            darkness: the stairwell: take it to electric: to
            piddle: to a pair of dank: a bed: a room:
            walls

They read:  prison if a baby fucks a baby: surprise: a
            baby: a stone in everybody's baby: baby

It was:     carved: hard: Larry said: Larry: a dream: a
            super hard fucking: no boner: all day

I saw:      broken frames: eyeglasses everyday: tape
            holding those: babies: a nose: flaring: a
            toad: a positive slope: the sine of what
            shitty is: such a full one: a commode

Which read: *pussy your dead*

I replied:  wish on a summer: fucking geometry:
            proofs: laterals: throw a punch or hum on
            the bus: cheer up my dear chin up:
            coughing: a basket a ball: dunk it: don't call
            me in the morning: in soft: in a lullaby

I asked:    what was sleep impossible temporary: or:
            how novel was family: is there only one right
            answer: for a taste of: what: is this tongue my
            milk its splatter some anger: what was it came

up pale: did you tear open every broken
locker: what slams: how this thing is: why it's
over: why it's done

He said:      who cares: who cares who cares: who: cares:
              who cares who: cares: who cares

## BIG PROBLEM SONNET

It was a big problem
losing his damn house keys
in the river of no memories.
The strident cry of his mom
cursing the red rooftops
dirtied the sky and the town bell
let roll one hell of a knell.
The sisters milked the tots
in the winter of their discount rent,
but they would not let him be
nine times his mama's pretty
boy thief of the ever-ruined
ladders in the drafty attic,
tears in his daddy's cataract.

## AFTER MANY YEARS OF LOOKING
## INTO A BUCKET OF WATER


I recall
a mother is
a deep
surprise like
an ocean
I've never seen
the Atlantic up
close but once
from a plane
the force of it
I could see
why through
a porthole
the eye eyes
it casts out
that is
what a mother means
each time
she splashes
on you

## FAMILY WHO ART IN THE VILLAGE
## THAT IS NOT BURNING DOWN


Family who art in the village that is not burning down.
Family who art in evenings the shade of the village that is
    not burning down.
Family who art in paintings in which many rags soaked in
    fuel will not catch fire.
Family who art a failure of fire but reeking of fire.
Family who art in a shiver the night-child makes when
    there is no fire.
Family who art great glad bells in the village that is not
    burning down.

Family who art not running from flaming parlors and
    combing their wild hairs.
Family who art not gone to bed on a flight of ashen stairs.
Family who art not up the torching tree in which the
    robin hatches a blue sky.
Family who art not taken to the bank in the belly of a
    tomcat.
Family who art not money that is burning like money.

# THEN, AGAIN

# IN LIEU OF HARTSHORN

We made from our children a town of criers.
We made from our mother a fountain of white-hot milk.
We staged on the square a drama of the blessed scalding.

We shook from the moon nine times the meteor showers.
We shook from the hare the blood of our quick-legged ilk.
We drew from the deck two jokers reveling.

We had from that day forth a comedy of fires.
We had from its pageant a showcase of charred steak.
We took to the blue-ribbon sky a great liking.

And we tried to stay awake.

# FAR FROM BAD AXE

There on the Thumb, at the edge of the silver-lipped lake, we were an eyelash fallen in the craw of the metal- mouthed implements, the mosquitoes flittering in the skin-tight aspen. Paper bark on the solstice, a poke in the eye with a stick, & there was nothing as heavy-handed as the heat. Swollen, a breeze planted the sassafras with smoke. I had run out of desire, divided our leg hair & combed it over the top of my head. Before dawn, my mother kissed me, a cigarette in her smile. She handed me a loaf of white bread. Wringing the jack-rabbit's neck was going to take every ounce of me. I couldn't help it if the butcher block of summer was carved by hunger. Half a mind of chokecherry & I hacked at the soft core of poisonous pulp. An arm, a leg, the tree traded limbs with me. At night, I grinded my intentions. I followed the curve of the moon & it set me straight.

## THE HOG FARMER'S DAUGHTER IS DANCING ON THE LAST NIGHT OF THE COUNTY FAIR

1

And if she follows me, fine.
We'll meet behind the corncob pile.

Tell her
where the white lies are.

2

As high
as an elephant's eye.

3

Red-handed, old man,
I have brushed my teeth again.

And the treetops have
caught the moon.
Our jocular one,
lowest of the low
lights in the mimosa,

God bless you

4

and keep you
my hopeful
heap of junk:

ribbons, bows,
tiny dismay.
Oh Boy,

it drags me
a long, long way.


5

Sugar tooth,
crude loot,

legumes, beans
in their black suits,

the rattle ripe,
the wind chime,

the wee shine.


6

It doesn't seem fair:

the whipped filly,
her matted hair,
the knot-tender,
his bad behavior.

*What have you done,*
he says to the horse.


7

a creep a crawl
these shoes need
some mending

at least the age of
disappointment
waxes as it gains

a stuffed animal
or a novelty tee
it doesn't matter

we just want to
bump bump
the bumper cars

# SHORT VERSIONS OF LONG STORIES

*(Sandy married a Dowell)*

Too pale
that thing
she hangs
her hat on

*(Ronald David married Joy)*

   A baby
at nineteen

   & later
there's another

   although
she only drove

   imports
flat out refusing

   to get
behind anything

   domestic—
all this & a little

   tennis
then twenty-seven

   years more
before divorcing

       & finally
taking her ass

    to Florida


*(Coleen Ann married John)*


tall as a tupelo
w/ rusted hair

his face like
a pink potato

but who knew
exactly what he did

for a living


*(Janet Sue married Kenny)*


a dead mom
then Vietnam

somehow
each one is

a common
problem

# AFTER THE NAMUR CURVE

If the wind didn't blow her skirt up again.
If the cottage windows didn't fog over.
If the zebra mussels didn't pile like china, like shatters of a
    shore party.
If the patriarchs didn't count their cribs
    out loud.
If the black-bottomed barges didn't look bored.
If the fox didn't untie a washed-up carp like a
    scarf, clawing it across the rocks.
If the red-headed stepchild didn't let the dog in.
If the catamaran didn't hold the bay at arm's length.
If the jib didn't hiccup.
If I weren't thinking of the slow-motion afterlife.
If my brother didn't play my grandfather's papery
    Panamanian bullhorn.
If he hadn't butchered the littlest bridge of the song.
If we weren't tighter than two coats of paint.
If I looked him in the eye and I didn't know why.

## A ROOM IN THE ELEPHANT

His children, both blonde, impossibly beautiful, like tender willows, they whip around the wide pasture. Hope sits on the swing, & this man, he pushes it higher. You wouldn't believe it if you saw it. Just look at them. We just look at them. I mean, would you just look at them?

# LIKE A MIRROR WHO GREW UP HERE

*for William Maxwell*

1
Born in: August: a suffering time:
golden light: fields: every last dog:
a thirst: a morning wet with dew:

2
Lived: on 9th: but moved: grew up
in a home: in what his father built:
east of Elm: north side of Park Place:

3
Wrote: of regrets: sadness: of friends
& murderers: the cruelty of the Spanish
flu: 1918: too much boyhood: too much
kindness: life in France: working with
Nabokov: bisexuals: the likes of John
Cheever: all that: nothing on Lincoln:

4
Moved: to Chicago: to Harvard: then
the years: New York: living in an East
Side Apt.: then Westchester: married
a Noyes: lady from Portland: Oregon:

5
Died short of ninety-two: years keen
on work: never thinking too much of
the factories: keeping his head at last
a bronze statue at the Library: a bust

## POEM IN WHICH EVERY LIVING THING
## HAS A HEART-SHAPED BOX INSIDE OF IT

my cousin
worked at
a box factory

folding time

between vodka
& the bad sadness
he turned

thirty or forty

a life
in prison
for what

someone's son

murder
a murderer
they said

what is a kid

what number
is it


&


I moved
to Portland
when I was 26

the river there
cut the city
in two sides

like an animal
flowing north
the Willamette

winds up with
the Columbia
which heads

to Astoria
& from there
into the Pacific

I couldn't believe it
*this world*
I said


&


I once built a box
a shipping crate
for a highly delicate
& intricately tooled
piece of machinery

it was headed
for Houston
or maybe Manassas
& eventually
into outer space

I was ashamed
my carpentry
was wicked
gross angles
no sense of scale

inside that box
the telescope
component was
a weird child
in a large coffin

after that
they never asked me
to build anything again

## SPACKLING

The plastic fill & mastic mesh.
A polish, a pursuit, the plumb
bob, & the proof. The stain &
loot, this loaf of, & rain. *Float:*
the ghost in the loam. A mix, a
measure, then a batch, then the
self-aggregate. A wand, or a
wash, a whopper. All that &
gravel, that is a rabble, a wall
pocked with sign: of hanging,
of genuine gruff, & groveling.

## POEM IN WHICH I COULDN'T FIND OREN'S HAT

because
he threw it
with all
the others
into the ring
of Podunk
that circle
in which
the misfits
cornered
by stories
lived out
prohibitive
old myths
I never did
see him in
a hat even
in winter
the shock of hair
like coal
it outlasted
him he died
a bad liver
a drunk
another one
added to
the low-level
figures

## ERSATZ DREAM NUMERO UNO

The father loping from the open face of a tunnel,
the night train made wholly more desperate for
how its rollicking doesn't satisfy, for how the
reverent systems bustle, muscle at once distorting
the shape of a thing, before restoring it, & the
conductor, pin-striped, pale-faced, the headlight
high beam wailing *make way, make way*—

# THE ALARM SIGNALS COMPANY

the backlog of 33,000 orders
when the factory opened in
1913 had something to do
with its demise in 1914 it re-
organized but closed by
1915 a bankruptcy it
made alarms sirens
electric horns auto
mobile horns rail
horns fire alarms
mine horns horns
for crossing others
these horns were
much easier no
need for power
or the steam
the whistle
always
needs

## ALL HANDS & THE COOK

*before Michelle died*

Alabastrine clouds were turning ashen.
They were always raining then.

All night long her muscles did twitch.
All night long her nerves did fidget.
All night long his ears did itch.

Always the things she said were said again:

*You try singing in this hailstorm*
*You try on this bag of bones like a fur coat*
*You try this having been a mother*

Inside him, her shipwrecked ghost.
In its possession, the noise of crows.

It's not the voice we praise the angels with.
It's not the voice he bathes the babies with.

It is his mouth washed out with soap.

It is his hair lost.
It is his basin clogged.
It is his hope. No,

it had to come to this:
her thumbnail paring found him
& ripped him from the cliff.

It mattered little what was hers.
Little what footing remained.

Did I mention that the boat had sunk?
That the fish had swum off?
That all his wishes had been drunk up?

But there was one last turnoff, mate.
One last plank.

It was time to take the garbage out.
Time to bite the lemon rind.

# THE MARSDEN CELLULOSE FACTORY

processed pulp

from cornstalks
to make

waterproof
linings

for battleships
the factory

touched
the sky

reaching
for the moon

for the far
away stars

tomorrow is
a dreamboat

taking off
like a straw hat

## A ROOM IN THE ELEPHANT

Already the big thing that was about to happen has happened, & my brother turns over in these mornings, like a new crop. He thinks he'll build an addition to the rib cage, &, in general, all of our spirits have redoubled. We do feel lucky, each of us knows why, but we know it separately. Recently, the dog got mixed up with the neighbor's dogs, &, ever since, I've had to tie him to the lower intestines. My dad says they keep him pretty good company.

# PORTRAIT OF A BOY RUNNING DOWN A HILL

*after Andrew Wyeth*

Hill like a wave, & the shadow
will not follow the boy, though

                wherever his father goes,
          his dying will follow—

              there's a pheasant hidden
        in the fence row, where hedge posts
           cast black hashes—& how

plainspoken is the snow.
It says: *I can't stay in this place*

            *one day at a time, boy,*
        *I know what you ride to:*

&#9733;


the father's car contorted,
        given to ghosts, to ashes,
not in the night, but in

           the harmonious brown
      winter, its endless barren

dormancy, that's what has
            pushed the boy to the front

      of the picture—I see him, all
floppy hat, green fatigues,
       running down Kuerner's hill—

&#9733;

as fast as a toy, he has
a shadow that isn't

      his own, this falling
boy flying from a man.

## HOW I LEARNED TO WORRY ABOUT
## THE FUTURE AS QUIETLY AS POSSIBLE

why out of
all the tools
in the garage
I chose it
something
its nature
its form
suggested
I was
in need so
I stole
my grandfather's
fretsaw I
put it under
my shirt by
my body
the small
boy like
a dream
I took it
home I
wanted
to cut to
the future
w/ a very
fine blade
I wanted
to see
if it lasted
one day

## COUGH CREEK

And then the well went
a mile a deep filled in by

tonnage babe the boards
split up my heart had no

floor of course it was
a forfeiture a gay-old

time a real bout of out
pouring I got so close

but I didn't come here
to enjoy it no my hands

both of them always
ongoing and on top of

their folding a misery
like a skeleton's yoga

bend it and debone it
I'm nobody's spleen

take that cool child
lay him out straight

only a peck of moon
but his face it shows

oh it just glows I said
suck these rainbows

from the ground up
and in the morning

walk to the flexible
aea and it will sing

bang-a-rainmaker
while blue goons

aim for the trees
if you ever have to

let a pretty thing go

# HENCE

# SIXTEEN PROLOGUES FOR EVERYDAY USE

In the beginning there were no words
for what the ocean was doing.

In the beginning the sky was just bits and pieces,
a seam, a torn-up sort of light, maybe
it never even completed a sentence.

In the beginning what we had were fragments,
every shard jutted out like a child.

In the beginning dangling was the only job
the tongue was cut out for,
so the waves went on licking the beaches.

In the beginning all of the petting was heavy.

In the beginning God said,
*are you going to eat that?*

In the beginning there was plenty of milk and cereal,
but no one was going to combine them.

In the beginning life was very hard
or worse than completely worthless,
and the people called it *diamonds*.

In the beginning one damn starling was a precious thing.

In the beginning a radio played,
and even if you came from the low animals
you got up and saluted.

In the beginning all day and all of the night
the tippy top of the sycamore swayed.

In the beginning paper rolled off reams,
but all the pictures of money were done by hand.

In the beginning there was a copy machine
out of which spilled the blueprint
for one tired mother, ten thousand thieves,
and the whole stupor of dads.

In the beginning the paint never dried.
Everything was still wet.

In the beginning it never boiled down,
nothing came to a head,
and nobody argued semantics.

In the beginning everyone was from Kentucky,
the rest were plucked from the rib of Jersey,

and when a heart got stuffed in a fool
it pumped broad daylight.

# I HAD A SILVER SOUL

I had a silver soul. It had four walls and a floor, and the unnamable names written all over its windows. I lived there, and if the sun rose, I didn't know. I couldn't get enough silver soul. I fell upon my knees and I begged the silver soul to go the movies. *Follow me*, I'd say, and then I'd lead the way to the car wash, through four quarters of basketball and onward to my grandmother's funeral. You would have been right if you had said my silver soul was like a monkey on my back, except it was a lot shinier, and that was off-putting to people who had the traditional monkeys on their backs and consequently did not have a silver soul to do whatever they wanted with. For instance, I threw little silver soul parties, just me, the silver soul, and a roasted leg of lamb. Maybe I put on a record or two. It grew late—well after the old house caught fire and my family ran off with another family—near dawn, but who could tell, and if I was putting on song after song, then I was putting on one more song for my silver soul and I was saying *Okay, silver soul, this is it, I promise,* but of course it was a lie. You couldn't fool a silver soul. Why would you even try to? I turned up the volume and I played the forgetful pretender. And just about anybody can do that.

# NOT RELUCTANTLY OR UNDER COMPULSION

I set the table
and I open up
the wardrobe.

I fashion
a grapevine chair
and I seat

the monarch—
I'm only
an upholder.

In the dark
I cut my hair
and I clean

the whole stove.
I prepare
potato pie

and I throw
my face
on a pillow.

I shut up
my eyes
but I see

my friends.
I pin them
like feathers

to my floppy hat
and I bring it
to the queen

like that.

# PORTRAIT OF A WOMAN LOOKING AWAY

*after Andrew Wyeth*

the distance
is a farm
two leaning
chimneys red
bricks driven
like sixteen-
penny nails
in the roof
& a pair
of pants is
possibly
tresses of
hair hung out
on a clothes-
line that's been
excited
by the blind
wind not to
mention how
the outhouse
is doghouse
the wagon is
tracks & in
the brown
grass splendor is
a pink dress
in a low plain
pasture &
high on the
hill's our
collected
reaching
for the things
we never did
brush against
the elbow

bone's arrow-
head the tough
rubber of
the bicep
like a green
garden hose
& all those
clapboards on
the house now
a washed-up
whale of gray
a dawn that's
not daylight
but still it's
today &
Christina
when I look
to you you
look away

## A ROOM IN THE ELEPHANT

I just close my eyes. I try to picture my brother working the crop with his bare hands, his determination to finger a thought in the nervous jelly, but that boat fails to float, so I get up & go wandering, through halls, past peepholes, & the next thing I know, I'm sleeping hard, my good ear to the dark meat of the sixty-pound heart.

# POEM IN WHICH ALL THINGS ARE EQUAL

Who laid down
the bouquet of beliefs.

I had held it
so long, lovingly.

Like an injury
who came to me—

I was falling, a corn crib,
breaking, a bird cage—

and who rang the bell,
but I could not,

I would not do.
Just look—

these weeds,
thistle pin pricks,

all of us
a scribbling curve.

I, sheared off
and who, the stalk,

the thought lost,
who had dreamed all of it up,

passed it through a sieve,
and there we were

a just-turned child,
a blur of bobwhite.

# THE CHORE

We gave the children the chore, but they threw the chore in the lake. When the children cut off our hair, they threw our hair in the lake, too, and the lake laughed quietly, quietly as a mirror, a mirror in which you had to look, and to look there was like looking under the bed skirt, which dressed our dreaming, and our dreaming was nothing if not the spackling on the original myth, but the myth was just a big bad big mistake, and that mistake had a name, a name carved in the crabapple on the horse's head, and that horse's head was a long face in a field of high grass far away from the aim of the arrow, and if the arrow pointed, it pointed to what was by then a ruined business, a business of dredging up old things like the summer in which the children had burned down the house, and the house when it was long enough underwater, underwater we could finally forget it, forget it had burned to the cold ground, the cold ground around which we marshaled our forces, forces we poured into the children, and the children, they were so holy.

## LIKE AN ASTRONAUT WHO HAS
## PLANTED A FLAG ON THE MOON

        sometimes
in a schoolyard

        tangled
in the yarn

        of these
old faces

        like fuel
a heart pours

        into space
its rocket

        lifts off
is spun up

        like light
a warp

    in the weave

        my mind
diagonals

        onward
its dutiful

        shuttling
to the future

        I wave
whenever

                    the past
recedes

            it leaves
a pinhole

            for my teensy
star spangles

## AT THE COOL CENTER OF MY DREAMING
## IS A SLIGHT CHANCE OF FIRE


Tucked there—into
the edge where too

thick a shade pales
the sedge—my truck

doors open, flap
steely flags. Automatic

bluegills bob whatever
snippet of crawler

I snare in the reeds.
The boy and the dad—

each opposed—reel
or unreel. I've worn

heavy boots. Weeping
willows do their thing.

For five bucks, the old
women split wet wood.

**Fire**, their signs say.
I shiver. The rib of a

dog moans. Shot through,
the wind is scrim. Then

green, all unshaven,
a beard of dangling

algae and, my heavens,
the bullfrogs in a gauze.

## TO A CHILD WHO DOESN'T UNDERSTAND
## WHAT HE'S GETTING INTO

Let's summon
the deep dark horses.
Let's marshal ten.
Julian,
let's drive them
into a square pen.
Let us rise,
like the rooftop
under which
we'll serve
a coltish family,
our hearts of straw,
this feeling, full-on
sharp, our shape,
the arc of a dart.

# THE CASKET FACTORY

i

The building was saved by
the firemen
& the sprinkling
system which poured
water down the south
wall but the wooden
water tower burned
to the ground

Firemen wetted
the galvanized
iron sheds
where the factory kept
its lacquer thinner

Had it gotten
hot enough
it would have been
a bomb

ii

Cousin Jerry Gibson reports
that his father Ted Gibson
then a member of the fire dept.
was slightly injured by this fire

iii

Ray Armbrust used to tell about
the time a Jacksonville undertaker
called w/ a special problem a very
elderly man was on his deathbed &
there was space left in a mausoleum
designed for older smaller coffins so
workers at the factory removed the
molding from a coffin to make it fit
& then sent it off & when Ray bumped

into the undertaker three years later
he asked "How did that coffin work?"
"We don't know" said the undertaker
"He healed up"

## LIKE A GUMBALL MACHINE

All our possibilities lie in eternity
in its bosom
the universe he means
it is the dispenser of all our joys
it is not wicked
like a gumball machine
it follows its own habits it sings
diligence it says
night is working society's
not impossible the moon up there
between it & us
the digits a clock blinking
weak light since it is the source of
our energies the home
of happiness like rain I like rain
I like clouds shall we not cling to it
praise it like seed like
a baby it vegetates so grandly
beans for the milk cow now you see
it's not for me
to blame it all this falling
for what it never did

## POEM ENDING WITH THE RETURN
## OF SPONTANEOUS CIRCULATION

I am a mother
or I am expecting
to be

you know what I mean by
*any minute now*

you said I'd like this
life given
the proper light

these thin clouds
caressing me in a pinch oh

it hurts though
sometimes it doesn't even
touch me

like a tornado
I wanted it to be

so definite yet
here we are     me &

this little-lighted
ephemera of mine     yes

that tired old song
a child sings

it massages me
into being

## BOBWHITE

Buckshot,
Thank God,
it got me not.
Farmer John,
a case of beer,
his boys, sure
as shit they hit
the broad side
of the barn.
Of course,
they swore
there were six
tits on a boar.
Whole hog,
summer's hot
hodge-podge:
bachelor button,
creeping jenny,
forget-me-not.

## JANUARY 33RD

I love how in the winter
nearly everything freezes,
or has frozen, & is now
starting to freeze again.

It's so cold my skin is
breaking, but I love
how my fingers begin
to bleed, on occasion,
the skin in extremis,

& when I do the dishes
for the umpteenth time,
like a steel-plated robot
scooting across Neptune,
I'm happy to report to you:

to feel is noble, a hope.
I love, too, how my heart
almost doesn't move,
or it doesn't want to.
How should I know

whether the blood is
pumping or if
the pipes are working
all right? I just love
a good confluence—

what is going, went,
what doesn't, won't.
It's hard to tell
I've been turned on,
but I love it anyway

how brainy ropes
coil in my vented
skull, how I am
a snake in a cave.
Of this, I'm sure:

I have two eyes
composed of coal.
I'm looking for you
out black windows.
What I see is a sight.

# SELF-INTERVIEW, WITH THEFT

As I get older I put
happens what you
too Flaubert sd that
is true though what
if I knew exactly
I would put it aside
I came home from
the house sat down
hat still on my head
rough statement I
didn't look at again
that page in general
in the dark true auto
the parts invented I
they never happened
come to their fathers
*So Long, See You*
somebody else's
evenly distributed
on the page my mother's
nothing more to say if
will be astonished I may
I do not think it will be
was faced with the difficult
sentences won't be sand
poem they hear
then they begin
there are strange
finally words last is
is in the hands of
know would you
you accept life is
unlucky you are you
to it I can't imagine
would have been so
I love if I hadn't been
awful

more trust in what
invent is important
whatever invented
the truth of it is
what I was doing
in favor of 1948
France I walked into
at the typewriter a
wrote a page a sort of
then thumbtacked &
until everything was on
the thing creeps a mole
biography is different
have trouble myself
young writers have to
mothers I meant
*Tomorrow* to be a story
tragedy the weight is
b/w the rifle shot
absence now I have
my mother turns up I
tell her to go away
necessary of course I
problem of self how
castles poets write a
the cadences in it &
humming in their ears
manifestations then
the words forgiveness
the injured not I don't
forgive me when
good no matter how
get firmer insight in
I really can't imagine I
deprived of everything
a writer it would've been
awful

# TO A MOONY STUKENBERG

*for my wife*

How I wish on a star, & you, or I, no,
we are both heir to the fruit of this
loop de loom, kin to the cold & gray-
gold, all the fail-fast glitter which is
woven—I suppose—through here,
right now, it is stitched into this body
I have up & flopped on the
Masquerader, where I wallow so
gravely it deranges the heavenly orbits,
fearful, I guess, of the way you stand
there too normally, putting one leg at
a time into your plain clothes, your
head in the brown hat that I can only
loathe, & at this impasse, at this peak,
which is really just the implacable
pressed into a small stone, there it is,
yes, gleaming in your eye, & now it's
getting biblical, the shimmer of the
histories is waning, & it's not too
beautiful, how Ruth is wedged
between Samuel & the Judges, forever,
& you should know that among the
mysteries, I'm only drifting, but from
this delicate, if not paper-thin air, I
gather there is a future to be written &
reflected on, a face, which is both
yours & mine, & it is ancient, as all
moon business is.

# GRAFFITI AT SUGAR CREEK

an arrow flies
into the cartoon heart
what else could
be said by force
by hand there's

a name for that
what's said on
paper on skin
for the profession
wrung from this

tiny love riven
written declared
sung or spat
it textures an echo
a report I hear

roll call it goes
Loretta Lavena
Oren Dietrich
Charles Carroll
all the Harmonys

& Abraham
his hat hangs up
like a folded man
his shirt his pants
all that emptiness

is for brothers for
each shape that says
how did I do
   did I fit in or
      do I go naked into


      the morning & see
   I'm like a suit
the whole time
   wearing
      *if I were if I were if I were*


      that chorus
   like a creek that's
barely there
   I put it on
      I chose to


      button it let it
   point me
to work to write
   to the bright
      center of heaven

# SOMETHING TO BE SAID OF PILGRIMS

on that boat which
sails out & how
inside of it
I return to form
again I loot the
moon there it is
caught in a cup in the
hull of your hands
bring it to
my face please
I insist
on a carriage ride me
to a land
where the events we
swim to
exist

# I ALWAYS WANTED TO LEAVE THIS TOWN

Away from here
           the near permanent
semi–soft
           peninsula that is
           my own
     personal
Florida

                    that is
           the cobbled together
           sinking hell
                    that is
           the stink of what was
                    that is
           what had touched on
           the tip of
           Ponce's tongue

★


when he whispered the word *fountain*
           it was precisely that
     but I'm not sure whether he heard
           a sound
           a faucet
           a thing
           the god
           forgot or
           left full
           on & open
           so long there was
           just no
           beginning
           to it

★

                    then not even
putting a finger on it      that is
                            our gift
let us open it here
                    after too long
                    in that florid
                    steaming mosquito
                    bog of dreams
                    who can say enough
                    goodbyes to it     not
                    me
                            I tear open
the paper but there is
                            nothing in there


★


            so I can't remember
what I wanted to say
            the words roll forward but
then they recede
            and that empty space is
almost
            its own newness
plain old youth gone to
            the waves to their
                    green acrylic sheets
to the sky's painted steel plate
                    its drinkable air its
                            near-blue not quite
                    a tincture
            for our chronic
                    dreaming


★

                    when
in that metro long ago
                         Ezra said
        *make it new*
                          he was already crazy dead *petals*
*on a wet black bough*
            so tired      a pounded nail      so tired
                 like that
                 a thing goes
                 bent over from
misuse
            a person is only      this shuffling
to and fro in its lightweight shoes      in its
                 positron conduction shirt


★


            I said look Ponce
the new car of living is going on
            somehow after all these endeavors after
                    a hundred years or more of
you know
                    just holding up the ladder
for that person we called      our father
            his set of directions so
                 illegible while
            our mother was just
                         hanging over
                         the whole enterprise
                         her wires tangled by
                         misapplications of
            desire like
                 crimson & clover
            the turning of love
                         over &      over


★

come back here now
and let me wash your hands
in this hot water
again        the whole country's headed down
south our blood going
burgundy gears whirling
our trees falling
just like everybody else's
in shadows        in black bars
beneath the wide eye of our burning
yellow star please
before we leave this town for good
let me stand here a minute
contented and
prisoner to it

# Acknowledgments

Thank you to the editors of the following journals,
where these poems first appeared, sometimes under different titles:

*Anti-:* "Bobwhite"

*Bateau:* "I Had a Silver Soul"

*Beecher's:* "To a Moony Stukenberg" & "Sixteen Prologues for Everyday Use"

*Caketrain:* "Far from Bad Axe"

*The Cincinnati Review:* "Cough Creek"

*Denver Quarterly:* "The Rope Advances"

*Diode:* "All Hands & the Cook"

*Ink Node:* "Poem in Which Every Living Thing Has a Heart-Shaped Box Inside of It", "Like an Astronaut Who Has Planted a Flag on the Moon", & "A Romantic in a Loose Land"

*M Review:* "The Hog Farmer's Daughter is Dancing on the Last Night of the County Fair", "At the Cool Center of My Dreaming is a Slight Chance of Fire", & "Some Birds Won't Fly"

*Mud Luscious Press Quarterly Online:* "A Hundred Thousand Hollow Legs"

*Nightblock:* "A Room in the Elephant", "Like a Gumball Machine", "Portrait of a Boy Running Down a Hill", & "Portrait of a Woman Looking Away"

*Paper Darts:* "Writing Larry Lingo"

*Parcel:* "Family Who Art in the Village That Is Not Burning Down"

*Prick of the Spindle*: "Not Reluctantly or Under Compulsion"

*Puerto Del Sol:* "In Lieu of Hartshorn"

*Sixty-Six: The Journal of Sonnet Studies:* "Big Problem Sonnet"

*Super Arrow:* "Poem in Which All Things Are Equal" & "Monologue after a Mostly Unapparent Kingdom Come"

+

Thank you to **Greying Ghost Press** for publishing the chapbook "In Lieu of Hartshorn", which included some of the poems from this manuscript.

+

Finally, thank you to the following writers who so encouraged and nurtured this collection of poems:

Jill Stukenberg, Lauren Genovesi, Stephen David Caldes, C. Parker Staley, Heather Herrmann, Misty Harper, Daneen Bergland, Emily Kendal Frey, Sara Brant Guest, David Bachmann, Stefan McKinstray, Casey Thayer, Michelle Boisseau, Connie Voisine, Kyle McCord, & Nick Courtright.

# Notes

"Henri Lamothe Dives from the Flatiron Building into Twelve Inches of Water": based on the reporting found in "Big Frog in a Small Pond," written by Edward Hoagland, published in *Sports Illustrated*, March 3rd (1975), as well as "Will Wet Sponge Be Next?" written by Steve Harvey, published in the *Milwaukee Journal*, May 10⁴ (1977). Henri Lamothe once held the Guinness World Record for highest dive, shallowest pool. At age 70, he successfully dived from a 40-foot ladder into 12 inches of water. The author's aunt married a nephew of Lamothe.

"The Kickapoo China Company": based on the reporting found in "Stetson China Company Was Moved Here from Roodhouse," published in *Lincoln Evening Courier*, August 26th (1953).

"The Love Manufacturing Company": indebted to the article "The Lincoln Automobile," written by Nancy Lawrence Gehlbach, published in *Our Times* (1998).

"The Alarm Signals Company": indebted to the article "A Factory Incubator," written by Nancy Lawrence Gehlbach, published in *Our Times* (2002).

"Marsden Cellulose Factory": indebted to the book *Lincoln, Illinois: A Pictorial History*, written by Paul E. Gleason, published by G. Bradley (1998).

"The Casket Factory": indebted to the article "Lincoln Casket Company," written by Nancy Lawrence Gehlbach, published in *Our Times* (2002).

"Portrait of a Woman Looking Away" & "Portrait of a Boy Running Down a Hill": inspired by the paintings *Christina's World* & *Winter 1946* by Andrew Wyeth. *Christina's World* depicts a woman, afflicted by polio, crawling through the grass. *Winter 1946* depicts a young boy dressed in army fatigues and running down a hill—the same hill on which Wyeth's father died in a car wreck.

"Self-Interview, with Theft": an erasure/found poem indebted to "The Art of Fiction No. 71," an interview with William Maxwell, conducted by John Seabrook, published in *The Paris Review* (1982).

# About Atmosphere Press

Atmosphere Press is an independent, full-service publisher for excellent books in all genres and for all audiences. Learn more about what we do at atmospherepress.com.

We encourage you to check out some of Atmosphere's latest releases, which are available at Amazon.com and via order from your local bookstore:

*I Would Tell You a Secret*, poetry by Hayden Dansky

*Aegis of Waves*, poetry by Elder Gideon

*Footnotes for a New Universe,* by Richard A. Jones

*Streetscapes*, poetry by Martin Jon Porter

*Feast*, poetry by Alexandra Antonopoulos

*River, Run!* poetry by Caitlin Jackson

*Poems for the Asylum*, poetry by Daniel J. Lutz

*Licorice*, poetry by Liz Bruno

*Etching the Ghost*, poetry by Cathleen Cohen

*Spindrift*, poetry by Laurence W. Thomas

*A Glorious Poetic Rage*, poetry by Elmo Shade

*Numbered Like the Psalms*, poetry by Catharine Phillips

*Verses of Drought*, poetry by Gregory Broadbent

*Canine in the Promised Land*, poetry by Philip J. Kowalski

*PushBack*, poetry by Richard L. Rose

*Modern Constellations*, poetry by Kendall Nichols

*Whirl Away Girl*, poetry by Tricia Johnson

# About the Author

Travis Nathan Brown was born in Lincoln, Illinois in 1980. He studied literature and writing at University of Missouri—Kansas City (B.A., 2003) and at New Mexico State University (M.F.A., 2006). His writing has appeared in a range of journals over the years, including *Fence, Salt Hill, West Branch,* and *Hayden's Ferry Review.* He is a Registered Nurse and works in psychiatry. He lives in Wausau, Wisconsin with his wife and son. *In the Village That Is Not Burning Down* is his first collection of poems.

CPSIA information can be obtained
at www.ICGtesting.com
Printed in the USA
LVHW092205300721
694164LV00004B/197